Camdean School

Item no. 01005

*Life in
Victorian Britain*

The Victorians
at Play

Rosemary Rees

First published in Great Britain by Heinemann Library
an imprint of Heinemann Publishers (Oxford) Ltd
Halley Court, Jordan Hill, Oxford OX2 8EJ

MADRID ATHENS PARIS FLORENCE PRAGUE WARSAW PORTSMOUTH NH CHICAGO
SAO PAULO SINGAPORE TOKYO MELBOURNE AUCKLAND IBADAN GABORONE JOHANNESBURG

Designed by Ron Kamen, Green Door Design Ltd, Basingstoke, Hampshire
Colour Repro by Track QSP Ltd, London
Printed in Spain by Mateu Cromo Artes Graficas SA

99 98 97 96 95
10 9 8 7 6 5 4 3 2 1

ISBN 0 431 06667 1 [HB]

99 98 97 96 95
10 9 8 7 6 5 4 3 2 1

ISBN 0 431 06683 3 [PB]

British Library Cataloguing in Publication Data
Rees, Rosemary
  Victorians at Play. - (Life in Victorian Britain Series)
  I. Title II. Series
  941.081

Acknowledgements
The Publishers would like to thank the following for permission to reproduce photographs:
Barnaby's Picture Library: p. 17B
Bridgeman Art Library: p. 13B
Christopher Wood Gallery: p. 21A
Courtesy of the Trustees of the V&A: p. 9B, p. 29B
The Illustrated London News Picture Library: p.19C, p. 22A, p. 24A
The Mansell Collection: p. 10A, p. 23B
The Mary Evans Picture Library: p. 7B, p.11C
Museum of London: p.14A
NRM/Science & Society Picture Library: p. 28A
The Raymond Mander and Joe Mitchenson Theatre Collection: p. 25B
Sotheby's Transparency Library: p. 26B
The Tate Gallery: p. 4A, p. 8A

Cover photograph © Courtesy of the Trustees of the V&A

Our thanks to Professor Eric Evans of the University of Lancaster for his comments in the preparation
of this book.

Weights, measures and money

Victorians used a system of weights and measures that is not the same as the metric system
we use now. The system the Victorians used is called the 'Imperial' system.

Imperial measures

Length
1 inch [2.5 cm]
12 inches (1 foot) [30.0 cm]
3 feet (1 yard) [1.0 m]
1,760 yards [1.6 km]

Capacity
1 pint [0.56 litres]
8 pints (1 gallon) [4.50 litres]

Weight
1 ounce (oz) [28 grams]
16 oz (1 pound 'lb') [.45 kg]
14 lbs (1 stone) [6.3 kg]
28 lbs (1 quarter) [12.75 kg]
4 qtrs (1 hundredweight 'cwt')
    [50.00 kg]
20 cwts (1 ton) [1 tonne]

Area
1 acre [0.40 hectares]

Money
4 farthings = 1 penny (1*d*)
2 halfpennies = 1 penny (1*d*)
12 pennies = 1 shilling
        (1/- or 1*s*)
20 shillings = £1

CONTENTS

1 Derby Day

Most Victorian people had very little free time. They worked long hours to earn a living. For many people it was a luxury to have any free time at all, and it was marvellous just to be able to stay in bed late, hang about on street corners or go out drinking.

However, during Queen Victoria's reign, working people did gradually manage to get more time off. In 1844 Parliament passed a Factory Act which said that women were not to work for more than twelve hours a day in textile **mills**. Thirty years later, in 1874, Parliament said that women and young people were not allowed to work in mills for more than ten hours a day.

The first bank holidays

In 1871 bank holidays began. Banks, factories, shops and offices closed. Everybody had a holiday. In 1886 Parliament passed the Shop Hours Act. This said that young people under the age of eighteen could not work for more than 74 hours a week. They could work for up to thirteen and a half hours on weekdays and six and a half hours on Saturdays. Victorians thought of Sundays as holy days. Although most working people had the day off, very little entertainment or fun was allowed.

Rich people had a different sort of problem about their free time. They had so much of it that they couldn't always find enough to do. In the country, the men hunted foxes, stags and otters; they shot pheasants and partridges, rabbits and grouse.

This picture is called *Derby Day*. It was painted between 1856 and 1858 by William Powell Frith. Look carefully and you will find lots of rich and poor people. Look even more carefully and you will see that rich people and poor people aren't actually mixing together. They are having fun separately.

They fished. In the towns they went to their **clubs**. These were all things men did. Rich women got involved in **charitable works** such as giving out soup to the poor; they visited their friends and relations; they read and sewed and painted. Many of them became extremely bored. However, the one day that rich people and poor people both enjoyed was **Derby Day**.

The Derby

In Victorian times the Derby was the most important horse race of the year. It was so important that **Members of Parliament** gave themselves a holiday for the day so that they could go. Everyone else who could get there wanted to go as well. Rich people went in carriages with their servants. They took hampers full of wine and chicken and puddings so that they could have an elegant dinner while they were there. Poorer people got there as best they could – by train, in open-topped buses or simply by walking. They took sandwiches or just loaves of bread and beer with them. It was a fun day out for everyone. Not everyone, of course, approved.

The Derby was held every June on Epsom Racecourse on the South Downs in Surrey. Horses raced along a flat grass track that was about a mile and a half [*three kilometres*] in length. The owner of the winning horse won around £250,000. The winning horse was then used for **breeding**. Foals from a Derby winner sold for a lot of money, and the owner became even richer. People, rich and poor, bet money on which horse would win. Some people made a lot of money. Others lost a lot. Apart from the betting, there were other ways of having fun. Look at the painting and see what you can find.

2 Hunting, shooting, fishing – and poaching

The rich

Many rich families owned **estates** in the country. For some families these estates included grouse moors in Scotland and North Yorkshire. Other families had certain rights which allowed them to hunt over Dartmoor and Exmoor in the West Country. Families owning estates in East Anglia, especially in the Fens, possessed marshes, streams and lakes.

This meant that rich families hunted, shot and fished in their spare time. They hunted foxes, otters, deer and hares. Usually they hunted on horseback and sometimes they had packs of **fox hounds** or **beagles** with them, too. They shot grouse, ducks, pheasants, pigeons and rabbits. They fished for salmon, trout and pike. They hunted and shot and fished for fun. Rich people sometimes made great occasions out of going hunting or shooting. They invited their rich friends and had a party afterwards.

The poor

Poor families living in the country needed rabbits, pigeons and pike for food. But they were not allowed to hunt and shoot and fish on rich landowners' estates. Some poor people got round this. The men and boys went **poaching**. They set secret traps and snares. They learned how to 'tickle' trout so that they could pick the fish from rivers and streams with their hands.

Poachers took a terrible risk. There were very strict Game Laws. Until 1857 poachers who were caught could be **transported** to Australia and would never see their friends and families again. After 1857 poachers were put in prison or made to pay heavy fines. If a poacher worked for the landowner, he would certainly lose his job. If a cottage went with the job, he would lose that, too, and his family would be homeless.

Source A

Most days we'd have a hare, or a pheasant he'd pick up a day or two after a shoot, and we'd wild duck sometimes, and I got trout out of the brook.

An old labourer told John Halsham that when he was a boy he lived with his father in the woods. This is part of what he said. John Halsham wrote it down in a book called *Idlehurst*, which was published in 1897.

Clearly they ate well. Not all poor country people were this lucky. Most of them were afraid of the Game Laws and the punishments if they were caught.

This picture is called *The Young Squire*. It was painted in the nineteenth century. Try to work out what the young squire has been doing, and whether anyone in the picture might be thinking about doing some poaching.

Until I was ten years old there were three of us, my sister being two years older and my brother two years younger than myself. He was my great chum: we took long walks and climbed trees and collected birds' eggs (we only took one out of each nest), and I can still feel the thrill of discovering a fresh egg to add to our collection, and the terror of thrusting my bare arm into a sand-martin's long, dark hole when there might be a peck from the bird at the end.

Not everyone living in the countryside had fun hunting, shooting or fishing! Mary Paley Marshall was the daughter of a country **rector**. She was born in 1850. When she was a girl she lived near Stamford in Lincolnshire. Later, she wrote about her life, in a book called *What I Remember*. This is what she remembers about playing in the woods and fields.

3 Village fun

At the beginning of Queen Victoria's reign village people had to make their own fun. A trip to the nearest town was out of the question for most villagers. This was because usually there was no transport. Villagers had to walk whenever they wanted to go anywhere. For most villagers, it would take far too long to walk to the nearest town and back again in an evening – and after a hard day's work. Sometimes a **circus**, a **fair** or some travelling musicians would pass by, and stop for a day or two. For most of the year, however, it was up to the villagers themselves to entertain their friends and families. Every village, no matter how small, organized its own leisure activities. These might be cricket, football, an orchestra or brass band, or amateur dramatics.

This picture is called *A Country Cricket Match*. It was painted by John Robertson Reid in the nineteenth century. Most of the villagers seem to be there: young people, old people and middle-aged people. They are not all playing cricket and some of them aren't even watching the game. But they are all enjoying themselves.

Village stations

By the 1860s, however, a very large number of villages were linked into the railway network. The Tewkesbury and Malvern line in Worcestershire, for example, linked villages along the way. It was opened in 1862 and in 1876 was joined to the Midland Railway. This meant that people could travel further more easily. They travelled to go to work. They also travelled to towns for an evening out.

   A grim little game often played by the younger children was called 'Daddy'. For this a ring was formed, one of the players remaining outside it, and the outside player stalked stealthily round the silent and motionless ring and chose another girl by striking her on the shoulder. The chosen one burst from the ring and rushed round it, closely pursued by the first player, the others chanting meanwhile:

Round a ring to catch a king
Round a ring to catch a king
Round a ring to catch a king

– and, as the pursuer caught up with the pursued and struck her neck with the edge of her hand –

Down falls Daddy!

At the stroke on the neck the second player fell flat on the turf, beheaded, and the game continued until all but one were stretched on the turf.

Flora Thompson was born in 1876 at Juniper Hill, a tiny village on the borders of Oxfordshire and Northamptonshire. She wrote about her childhood there in a book called *Lark Rise*, which was published in 1939. Here she describes one of the village games.

This picture is called *Returning from the Fair*. It was painted in 1837 by Thomas Webster. It shows villagers coming home after a typical village fair, which you can see to the left of the picture.

4 Travelling shows

Source
A

This picture of people enjoying a travelling fair was painted by Percy Cruickshank at the very beginning of Queen Victoria's reign.

In Victorian times there were all sorts of shows and entertainments travelling the country. There were **fairs** and **circuses**. There were animal shows with dancing bears, elephants and camels. There were Punch and Judy shows and men playing **barrel organs**, sometimes with a real live dancing monkey on top. Actors travelled around and put on plays in tents and village halls. Not all the shows were good and not all the audiences liked what they saw. But for many working people and their children, these travelling shows brought some fun into their hardworking lives.

Source
B

At 6 o'clock the wild beasts were ready and we all went to the show. There was a lion and a decent wolf. A laughing hyena set us all off laughing. A black sheep in the pangs of hunger was bleating piteously. There was no bicycle. The ground was in a swamp with pools of water, and huge gaps of canvas overhead let in the pouring rain.

Francis Kilvert was born in 1840. He was a curate at Clyro in Radnorshire and then vicar of Bredwardine by the river Wye. Between 1870 and 1879 he kept a diary. This is part of what he said about a visiting show.

Source C

These children, and some adults, are watching a Punch and Judy show on a street corner in London. The photograph was taken in 1900.

Punch and Judy were puppets. The person giving the show set up a little theatre. He then got inside so that he could not be seen. He held up Punch and Judy so that the children could see them. He made the puppets act. He spoke for them with lots of different voices. As well as Punch and Judy, there was usually a baby and sometimes a dog in the stories. Whatever the story, Punch always ended up screaming with anger and hitting the other puppets. The baby was usually dropped many times.

Source D

The various members of Sleary's company gathered. There were two or three handsome young women among them, with their husbands and their children. All the fathers could dance upon rolling **casks**, stand upon bottles, catch knives and balls, twirl hand basins, ride upon anything, jump over anything and stick at nothing. All the mothers could (and did) dance, upon the slack wire and the tight-rope, and perform rapid acts on bare-backed horses.

Charles Dickens wrote a lot of stories about people living in Victorian Britain. One of them was called *Hard Times*. It was published in 1854. In it he describes a circus. This is part of what he says about the people in a circus company run by Mr Sleary.

5 May Days and Whitsun walks

Victorian children who lived in villages in the country had special celebrations on **May Day**. Victorian children who lived in towns had special celebrations at **Whitsun**. Adults helped the children get ready for these great days, but they did not take part.

May Day

For hundreds of years country people had made May Day a special day. In some villages there were maypole dances; in others, there were special games and sometimes the villagers acted a play. In all villages, the villagers chose a girl to be 'May Queen'. She was crowned with flowers and was queen for just one day – May Day, which was always 1 May.

In Victorian times most villages kept the old custom of 'garlanding'. Village girls and boys made a May Day garland. They collected hundreds of flowers and wove them around a wooden frame. The frame was shaped like a bell and was usually about 1,300 centimetres high. When the garland was finished all the village children put on their best clothes. They then walked in a **procession**, carrying the garland carefully.

First they stopped at the vicar's house and then at the **squire**'s house. Then they walked round all the other houses in the village and the farms outside the village. Whenever the children stopped at a house, they sang a song and were usually given some money. When it was all over, they tramped back to the village where the adults had a huge tea ready for them in the village hall or schoolroom.

Whitsun

Most **industrial** towns, like Bolton and Bury in the north of England, had Whitsun Walks. These were organized by local Sunday Schools. Each Sunday School had its own beautifully embroidered banner. Every Whitsunday the children gathered outside their own Sunday School. They wore their best clothes. They lined up behind their Sunday School banner and went on a procession around their town. They were joined by children from other Sunday Schools. Soon all the Sunday School children in the town were in one procession, marching behind their own banners. At the end, tea and sticky buns were provided for everyone.

Source A

Good morning, ladies and gentlemen, it is the first of May,
And we are come to garlanding because it's new May Day;
A bunch of flowers we've brought you, and at your door we stay,
So please give us what you can and then we'll go away.

This is one of the many May Day songs sung by village children in the nineteenth century.

A painting from about 1860, showing children setting off for a May Day celebration.

On the last morning in April the children would come to school with bunches, baskets, arms and pinafores full of flowers – every blossom they could find in the fields and hedges or beg from parents and neighbours. Some of the bigger boys walked six or eight miles [*ten to thirteen kilometres*] to a distant wood where primroses grew. These, with violets from the hedgerows, cowslips from the meadows and wallflowers, oxlips, and sprays of pale red flowering currant from the cottage gardens formed the main supply. In time the wooden frame was covered, even if there had to be solid greenery at the back. While the children made the garland, an older girl, perhaps the May Queen herself, would be busy in a corner, making the crown. This always had to be a daisy crown. Meadow daisies were too common, and so red and white garden daisies were used, with a background of dark, glossy, evergreen leaves.

Flora Thompson, who was born in 1876, remembers May Day in her village of Juniper Hill. You can read more about Flora Thompson on pages 9 and 26.

6 Pleasure gardens and garden parties

Source
A

Pleasure gardens

Most pleasure gardens began as public house gardens. People sat in the pub garden and drank beer or gin, and ate jellied eels, shrimps or whatever the pub had to offer. They could also drink tea. Some were quite large. At some, people could listen to music, dance or watch fireworks. In London at the Hippodrome, Notting Hill, there was a miniature racecourse, while at the Red House, Battersea, visitors could shoot pigeons. Some pleasure gardens were places where people could go with their families to have some fun. Others were places where no respectable person would dare to go.

This picture, called *The Dancing Platform at Cremorne Gardens*, was painted by Phoebus Levin in 1864. Cremorne Gardens was a pleasure garden in King's Road, Chelsea. It was the largest London pleasure garden, and was very popular. As well as eating and drinking, visitors could watch, and take part in, all kinds of entertainments. There were theatres and side-shows, fortune tellers, tightrope walkers, shooting galleries and circuses. There was a ballroom for 4,000 people, and smaller dancing platforms. However, pick-pockets and other criminals went there, too. Local people began to complain. The Cremorne Gardens were closed down in 1877.

Garden parties

Rich and well-off people often held parties in their gardens. Sometimes these parties were just for fun. Aunts, cousins, brothers, sisters and friends came over to eat under the trees and play tennis or cricket or **croquet** afterwards.

Other garden parties were more serious. The rich men and women who gave them wanted to get different sorts of people to meet. They wanted artists and architects to meet people who might perhaps pay for their pictures and designs. They wanted actors and authors of plays to meet with people who could provide the money to have their plays performed. These rich people wanted to influence what happened.

Source B

A joint of roast beef, a joint of cold boiled beef, 2 ribs of lamb, 2 shoulders of lamb, 4 roast fowls, 2 roast ducks, 1 ham, 6 medium sized lobsters, 1 piece of collared calf's head, 18 lettuces, 6 baskets of salad, 6 cucumbers, stewed fruit and three or four **dozen** plain pastry biscuits, two dozen fruit turnovers, four dozen cheese cakes, 2 cold cabinet puddings, 1 large Christmas pudding, a few baskets of fresh fruit, three dozen biscuits, a piece of cheese, 6 lb butter, 4 loaves of household bread, three dozen rolls, 6 loaves tin bread, 2 plum cakes, 2 pound cakes, 2 sponge cakes, a tin of biscuits, $\frac{1}{2}$ lb tea.

Victorians also went on picnics! In 1861 Mrs Beeton wrote a cookery book. This is part of what she said would be needed for a picnic for forty people.

Source C

This picture of a garden party was drawn in 1875. The garden party was in the garden of Holland House, in London. Lady Holland gave parties like this for rich and well-off people who were involved in politics.

7 Lectures, libraries, art galleries and museums

Many Victorian men and women wanted to find out more about the world around them. They spent a lot of their spare time doing this. They went to lectures on science and religion, history and exploration. They listened to authors like Charles Dickens reading from books they had written. They listened to politicians like William Gladstone, who could speak for three or four hours at a time. They borrowed books from libraries and visited art galleries and museums.

Free libraries

In 1845 Parliament said that local **councils** could set up free libraries if they wanted to. In 1852 the very first free library opened in Manchester. Soon other cities set up libraries of their own. People who did not have the money to buy books could now read as many books as they wanted to. They also read magazines like the *Penny Magazine*, the *Family Economist* and the *Mechanics' Magazine*. They read newspapers like the *Echo* which only cost a halfpenny. Magazines and newspapers like these were published especially for working people.

By the end of Queen Victoria's reign in 1901, there were many more art galleries, concert halls and museums than there had been at the beginning. Many were in London. Londoners looked at paintings of famous British people in the National Portrait Gallery, which was opened in 1896.

A year later they flooded into the Tate Gallery to look at paintings and drawings from all round the world. In 1899 work began on the Victoria and Albert Museum in South Kensington, London. It was built opposite the Natural History Museum.

Cities like Leeds, Manchester and Birmingham quickly copied what was happening in London. Soon every large city in Britain had its own art gallery, museum and concert hall. They competed with each other to have the biggest and the best.

Source A

8 September 1881
I shall soon take my first lesson in shorthand writing, and in which I hope to become an efficient writer. There are two classes, namely Elementary and Advanced. I have been a subscriber to Cassell's *Popular Educator* since 1880, with a view to the advancement of my education, and which I am glad to say has done a great deal for it. I also subscribe to a new paper called *Peoples of the World*. They come out monthly.

James Turner was born in 1857. He lived mostly in Halifax, Yorkshire. The job he had longest was as a driver of a horse and cart. In June 1881 he began keeping a diary. This is part of what he wrote.

This drawing of the inside of a working men's **club** was made in 1870. These clubs began in the 1850s and 1860s. At these clubs working men could read books and newspapers. They could play games like billiards in a quiet atmosphere. Many working men went to their local working men's club instead of going to their local pub.

Few of the working class could afford the luxury of a weekly paper in their own home; they began the system of 'clubbing up' by several families in order to buy and make one paper enough for a large circle of readers. It was not unusual for a single paper to be used by an entire village.

William Scruton wrote a book called *Pen and Pencil Pictures of Old Bradford*. It was published in 1891. This comes from his book. He is explaining how working-class people managed to buy newspapers.

At the beginning of Queen Victoria's reign newspapers were expensive. This was because they were taxed. There was a stamp duty of 4d on each paper, an advertisement duty of 3s 6d on each advertisement and a duty on the paper on which the newspaper was printed. This meant that newspapers cost around 7d a copy. By 1861 Parliament had stopped all of these taxes. Newspapers became much cheaper and many more were published.

8 Sport: football and cricket

People have played football for hundreds and hundreds of years. All they needed was a reasonably flat space, something to mark out goal posts and something to kick around. Boys, and sometimes girls, played football in fields and market squares, in back streets and yards. Each village had its own rules which everyone in the village knew and understood. Each back street had its own rules, too. Problems came when one village team or one street team played against another. Then the players had to agree the rules in advance.

Football gets organized

In Victorian times football was properly organized for the first time. So were other games like rugby, cricket and tennis. In 1863 some men who were very interested in football got together and called themselves the Football Association. They wrote down a set of rules which they wanted everyone who played football to follow. Gradually all the football clubs in the country agreed. One problem was to do with the footballs the teams used. In order for the game to be fair, the balls had to be the same size and they had to weigh the same. Factories began making leather footballs of the same size and weight in the 1870s.

By 1885 all football clubs were following the same rules and playing with the same sort of football. There were professional footballers, too.

These were men who were paid to play the game. Most professional football clubs were in the midlands and the north of England. More and more people went to watch football matches in their spare time. Towards the end of the century, as you have read, people had more spare time than ever before. They also had more money to spend.

Source A

In November came pig-killing time. Soon our ears would be tormented with the screams of the dying pig. Then the pig was washed and cleaned. As children we hung around waiting for the bladder which, when drained, we blew up with a clay pipe stem and then used as a football.

In 1973 a book was published called *Voices of Children*. This is what one old man remembered about getting a football when he was a boy.

Source B

It is surely possible that some who take an interest in the young would be glad to give a few hours on Saturday afternoons for the purpose of arranging a game of football. As things now are, some youngsters prowl about the streets eating rotting fruit and doing themselves no good in any way.

This is part of a letter. It was written in 1882 by some parents who lived in Brighton. They wrote to the people who ran the local School Board. They wanted the School Board to do something to get children off the streets at weekends.

In this picture, Blackburn Rovers are playing Notts. County at Kennington Oval. It is a Football Challenge cup match. The match was in March 1891. The picture was drawn in 1891 and published in a magazine called *The Illustrated London News*.

Cricket

Cricket, like football, is an old game. At the beginning of Queen Victoria's reign it was a rough sort of game. People played cricket on village greens. They played with curved bats and bowled underarm. There were no real rules that were used everywhere in the country. However, boys at **public schools** like Rugby and Eton began to play cricket. They also played cricket after they left school. Playing cricket gradually came to be something that a gentleman did. They played in special clubs and in county teams. It was some time before ordinary boys began playing cricket in the back streets.

Source D

Manly sports played as they should be played tend to develop unselfish pluck, determination, self-control and public spirit. Watch a group of School Board cricketers. No one quarrels with the placing of the field. They have learned to play the game.

Some school teachers thought that team games made their pupils into better people. This is what one teacher believed.

19

9 Women join in: tennis and cycling

Tennis

In 1874 a new game was invented by Major Wingfield. He called it 'sphairistike'. The game quickly became very popular. In 1877 the game was officially called 'lawn tennis'. The All England **Croquet** and Lawn Tennis club took over. They set up new rules and organized competitions, called tournaments. The most famous tournament was held at their own club in Wimbledon, south London.

Tennis was mostly played by the rich and well-off. This was because, to play the game, a person needed a racquet and tennis balls. These cost money. They also needed some flat grass on which to play, and a tennis net. Rich and well-off people held tennis parties in their own gardens. The men usually wore trousers called knickerbockers. These came to just below their knees. They wore stockings and lace-up shoes, and shirts. The women usually managed to hitch up their dresses a little so that they could run. They wore coloured scarves as belts. Sometimes they wore aprons over their dresses. They put spare tennis balls in their apron pockets. They usually wore little straw hats when they were playing.

Most rich and well-off Victorians thought that tennis was a respectable game. They let men and women play together. It was one of the few sports where this was allowed.

Cycling

Bicycles were invented in Victorian times. The first cycles were called 'velocipedes'. In 1868 a French velocipede, called the 'Michaux', began to be made in Britain. Hundreds of young men bought them. These velocipedes had two wheels, one behind the other, with a saddle in between. The front wheel was larger than the back one. There were pedals on the front wheel. The velocipedes were made from iron. They did not have any tyres, springs or brakes. They were very uncomfortable – and dangerous!

The 'penny-farthing' bicycle was supposed to be a safer sort of bicycle. It had a front wheel which was about 160 centimetres in diameter. The back wheel was only 30 centimetres in diameter. The cyclist sat on a saddle above the enormous front wheel. Getting on and off was very difficult.

Cycles for women

Women couldn't ride velocipedes or penny-farthings and still stay 'respectable'. They would probably have shown their legs as they got on and off. Victorians thought this was very rude indeed. However, in 1876 H.J. Lawson invented a bicycle with much smaller wheels and a comfortable saddle. It was called a 'safety' bicycle. It looked a bit like a modern bicycle. Women could ride it and still be thought respectable. Men and women joined new cycling clubs all over the country.

At the club house, after a ride through the lanes of Cheshire or over the Derbyshire hills, we ate an enormous tea of ham, pickles, jam and cake of such solidity that we called it a 'tram-stopper'. Washing-up followed, after which we cleared the tables away for either a meeting, a play or a concert, finishing the evening with dancing. By ten o'clock we were shooting down Schools Hill, bunches of wild flowers tied to our handle-bars, apples in our pockets, the wind lifting our hair.

Stella Davies was born in the second half of the nineteenth century. When she was a young woman she joined the Clarion Cycle Club. It was a club in Bradford, Yorkshire. This is part of what she remembered about the cycling trips she had with the Clarion Club.

This picture is called *The Tennis Match*. It was painted by Horace Henry Lauty in 1888.

Our girls have welcomed new outdoor sports and taken to many new indoor pastimes. Lawn tennis has apparently reached its maximum. Croquet, which was once out of fashion, seems to be reviving. Golf, one of the oldest games, has made a sudden leap in popularity and no book on pastimes would be complete these days without an article on cycling. Even cricket is now deemed suitable for girls.

This is from a magazine called T*he Girls' Home Companion*. It was published in 1895.

10 Music halls, theatres and magic lantern shows

Many Victorians loved watching actors, singers and dancers. Theatres and music halls, however, were built in towns and cities. Victorians who lived in the countryside couldn't always get to the big towns because it was difficult for them to travel out of their villages. They watched plays and shows put on in by travelling actors in their local village hall or schoolroom.

Theatres

By the end of Queen Victoria's reign, every large town and city had at least one theatre. Some theatres, like the Lyceum in London, put on serious plays. At the Lyceum Londoners watched Henry Irving act Shylock and Ellen Terry act Portia in *The Merchant of Venice*, by William Shakespeare. Other theatres put on very dramatic plays, full of murders and excitements.

Music halls

Music halls were different. Shows at music halls were full of singing and dancing. Some of the songs were very rude, some were funny and some were serious. Most music halls had a bar with bar maids to serve drinks.

Some Victorians, however, thought that acting of any kind was wrong. They disapproved of actors, singers and dancers. They disapproved of anyone who went to theatres or music halls.

Source A

These are pictures of the Royal Victoria coffee palace and music hall, in London. They were drawn in 1880.

This picture of a magic lantern show was drawn in 1858. Many Victorians watched magic lantern shows. The showman brought his 'magic' lantern to a rich family's home, to a school or to a village hall. The lantern shone a light that was powered by gas or oil. The showman moved photographs or painted pictures in front of the light. These pictures were projected on to a white screen. The pictures told a story.

Source **C**

Miss P. and two young gents going to the play at Drury Lane. The old Lady treated me to see it. The first part was Cinderella. I saw her in the kitchen among the cinders, and saw the witch turn her into a lady and make a carriage out of a pumpkin, four horses out of white mice, a coachman out of a rat, two footmen out of grasshoppers. This was done by the stage opening and the real things being pushed up by people below and the rat, mice and pumpkins and things being pulled below at the same time. Saw Cinderella go to the ball and lose her slipper and in the end she was married to a Prince.

William Tayler was a servant. He kept a diary in 1837 when he was working for a rich widow. She was called Mrs Prinsep. This is part of what he wrote on 27 January 1837. He wrote about a visit to Drury Lane theatre.

11 Public houses and 'song and supper' rooms

Rich and well-off people drank wine, gin, brandy and whisky in their own homes and in their **clubs**. Poorer people went to one of the hundreds of public houses, beer shops, gin shops and **gin palaces**. They could drink there, or take a jug of beer or gin home with them. They were open in the day and in the evenings. Some poor families spent up to half of what they earned on drink. Perhaps they did this because it was the only chance they had to have some fun. Perhaps they did this because they wanted to forget how awful their lives were.

This is a picture of a gin palace. It is a Sunday afternoon. The artist sat in the gin palace and drew what he saw. This picture was printed in a magazine called *The Graphic* in 1879.

Public houses

Public houses did far more than serve drink. People went there to gamble, too. They bet on games of skittles, on boxing matches, on **cockfights**, dog fights and rat-catching. They bet on almost anything. Many football and cricket clubs were based in a local pub. In 1865 there were thirteen football clubs in Sheffield. Eleven had local pubs for their addresses.

Drunkenness

Many Victorians were very worried about the amount of beer and alcohol the poor and working-class people drank. In London in the 1860s, 17,000 people a year were arrested for drunkenness. Church leaders and businessmen tried to do something about it. They started clubs like the Good Templars and the Band of Hope.

This picture of a 'song and supper' room was drawn in 1859. Some better-off people went to 'song and supper' rooms instead of the pub. There they could have a good meal and plenty to drink. They could watch actors singing and dancing. Sometimes they joined in the songs.

These clubs encouraged men, women and children to stop drinking alcohol. They encouraged children and adults to sign a promise, called the 'Pledge'. This was a promise that they would never let alcohol pass their lips. In 1871 the Liberal government said that children under the age of sixteen were not allowed to drink gin in a pub or gin palace. In 1882 pubs were forbidden to sell beer to children under the age of thirteen. Gradually, working people drank less and less alcohol.

12 Games and toys

Country children and town children, rich children and poor children all played games. Rich children, however, had more time to play than poor children. Their parents bought them expensive toys, too. But all children had fun when they could with the toys and games they had.

This picture is called *A Game of Marbles*. It was painted in the nineteenth century by William Bromley.

Source A

The village boys were champion marble players and thought nothing of walking five or six miles [*eight to ten kilometres*] on a Saturday to play with the boys of other villages and replenish their own store with their winnings. Some of them owned the scarce and valued glass marbles, called 'alleys'. These were of clear glass enclosing bright, wavy, multi-coloured threads, and they looked very handsome among the dingy coloured clay ones.

The girls skipped with any odd length of rope, usually their mothers' old clothes line. 'Dibs' was a girls' game, played with five small, smooth pebbles, which had to be kept in the air at the same time and caught on the back of the hand.

Flora Thompson was born in 1876 at Juniper Hill, a village on the Oxfordshire-Northamptonshire border. When she was old she wrote down her memories of her childhood. This is part of what she wrote about the games played by village children.

Source B

HINDE'S GRATIS PICTURE TOY BOOK.
(PROTECTED BY ROYAL LETTERS PATENT.)
MISS DOLLIE DAISIE DIMPLE,
AND HER TRUNK OF SMART CLOTHES ALL
TO TAKE ON AND OFF.
Everybody is pleased with this
Wonderful Shillingsworth.
FIFTY-FOUR
ARTICLES
Messrs. HINDE, 1a, City Road, London, E.C. WORKS, BIRMINGHAM & PARIS.

It consisted of tying a rope around a lad's body, fastening the other end to the door of any house, leaving some yards of slack rope, then giving a rat-tat-tat on the door. When the inmates tried to open it, the boy with his long leverage was as powerful as they; the door would open and shut, to the great amusement of the boys. When this see-saw had gone on long enough the rope was cut and the Long-tailed Pony was free, scampering away with the rest of us.

George Ratcliffe describes a game called 'Long-tailed Pony'. He played it when he was a boy in the east end of Leeds. He was born there in 1863. In 1925 he wrote a book about his life. It was called *Sixty Years Of It: Being the Story of My Life and Public Career.*

Girls from rich families played with dolls like this. This doll was called Miss Dollie Daisie Dimple. She had sets of clothes which could be taken on and off.

13 The seaside

At the beginning of Queen Victoria's reign, only rich people went to the seaside on holiday. It cost a lot of money to pay for a private carriage to take a family, their servants and their luggage to the seaside.

Railways made all the difference. In the 1840s working people started to go to the seaside for the first time. In the north of England, factories and **mills** closed down for **Wakes Weeks**, when everyone had a holiday. Families saved hard for a week away from home. They went by train to seaside towns like Blackpool. In other parts of the country, trains took working people to Scarborough, Ramsgate, Southend, Bournemouth, Broadstairs and Skegness.

Many holiday-makers stayed in **boarding houses**. In most seaside towns these were close to the new **promenades** and to the **pier**. **Landladies** managed the boarding houses. They saw that the visitors were comfortable and had the sort of food they were used to. Some visitors stayed in **rented** houses and rooms.

This poster advertises a railway journey from London to Hastings and Eastbourne in 1901, which cost 5 shillings.

Blackpool was a town that grew because of railways. More and more boarding houses were built and so were some hotels. In 1863 the North Pier was built so that people could walk out over the sea. In 1896 a giant wheel was put up. This was the start of the pleasure beach where people had fun at a **fair**.

Once a year, during Wakes Week, when the mills closed down, the Rossendale valley was all but deserted. Wakes Weeks are staggered, each town in the **industrial** area taking different weeks throughout the summer for their holiday. Most people went to Blackpool, though some went to Morecambe or even Rhyl. Blackpool, therefore, was full at any one time, with neighbours from the same town and no one need feel isolated or lonely. Groups of relatives would share lodgings or take them in the same street and young and old, children, courting couples and sober married folk alike, would spend a year's savings in one glorious spree.

Stella Davies remembers holidays from when she was a child. She was born in 1895 in Higher Crumpsall, near Manchester.

This is a photograph of people paddling at Yarmouth in 1892. When Victorians actually went swimming in the sea, men and women had to use different parts of the beach. Women went into bathing machines to change into swim suits. Bathing machines were little wooden huts on wheels. When the women had changed, the bathing huts were pushed into the sea. They could then have a swim without anyone seeing their bare legs or arms.

GLOSSARY

barrel organ A musical instrument on wheels looking rather like a piano but with a handle that is turned to make music. When someone turns the handle at the right speed, a cylinder turns inside the barrel organ and metal studs hit pipes or keys to make a tune.

beagle a dog, looking like a small fox hound, used to hunt hares

boarding houses houses, usually at the seaside, where people could rent rooms for a holiday

breeding mating animals so that they produce the sort of young that the owner wants – horses that run fast or jump well; cows that produce a lot of milk or sheep that produce good wool

cask a barrel

charitable works helping the poor and needy

circus a travelling show with animals, clowns and acrobats

club a place where gentlemen could go to read the papers, talk to other gentlemen and have a meal

cockfight Two cockerels (male chickens) were set against each other to fight until one of them killed the other one. People betted on which one could win.

council people elected to run a town

croquet a game played on grass where players have to hit balls through hoops with wooden mallets

curate a person who helps a parish priest

Derby Day a day in June when the Derby, a horse race, was run at Epsom on the South Downs

dozen twelve

estate land belonging to a rich person

fair Where people get together to trade things, like horses. Often there are entertainers and people selling food there too.

fox hound a dog specially trained to hunt foxes

gin palace a fancy sort of pub where different types of gin were sold

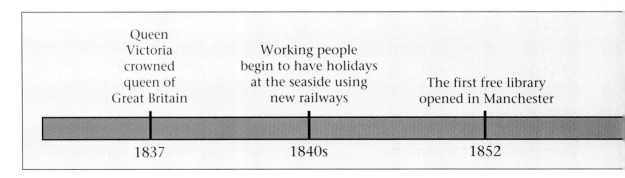

Queen Victoria crowned queen of Great Britain	Working people begin to have holidays at the seaside using new railways	The first free library opened in Manchester
1837	1840s	1852

industrial connected with industry

landlady a woman who owns, and then lets out, rooms

May Day a country festival held on 1 May

Member of Parliament a person elected to the House of Commons to represent all the people living in a certain area called a constituency

mill type of factory where things such as cotton were made

pier a long platform built out into the sea so that people could walk over the sea and look back at the land

poaching stealing game (venison, hare, duck, for example)

procession a long line of people walking together

promenades special pavements for walking along by the side of the sea

public schools the most important and well-thought of boarding schools for boys

rector a parish priest

rented a house or cottage or rooms for which money is paid on a weekly or monthly basis by the people who want to live there

school board school boards were set up by the Education Act of 1870; they were groups of people who were chosen to run board schools

squire a country gentleman

transported sent to another part of the world ruled by Britain, and not allowed to come back

Wakes Weeks certain weeks in the summer when factories and mills in the north of England shut down so that their workers could have a holiday

Whitsun the seventh Sunday after Easter

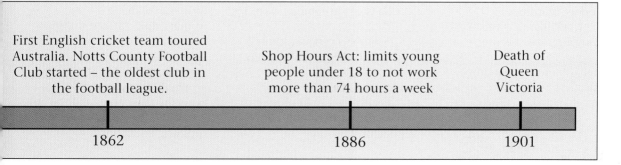

First English cricket team toured Australia. Notts County Football Club started – the oldest club in the football league.

Shop Hours Act: limits young people under 18 to not work more than 74 hours a week

Death of Queen Victoria

1862

1886

1901

INDEX

Plain numbers (3) refer to the text and written sources. Italic numbers (*3*) refer to a picture.